THE D- POEMS OF JEREMY BLOOM

A Collection of Poems
About School, Homework, and Life
(sort of)

Other Books by GORDON KORMAN

THE D- POEMS OF JEREMY BLOOM

A Collection of Poems
About School, Homework, and Life
(sort of)

GORDON KORMAN
and
BERNICE KORMAN

SCHOLASTIC INC.

New York Toronto London Auckland Sydney

ISBN 0-590-44819-6

12 11 10 9 8 7 6 5 4 3 2   2 3 4 5 6/9

Printed in the U.S.A.   40

First Scholastic printing, September 1992

Book design by Laurie McBarnette

For Charles Isaac Korman,
who prefers rear-wheel drive

CONTENTS

INTRODUCTION

The poetry in this book happened by mistake. The mistake was made by Jeremy Bloom, who is an expert mistake-maker.

It began with Jeremy's infamous alarm clock. Since the day he took it apart to try to make the world's first time-operated slingshot stink-bomb, it hadn't been working too well. It went off at three A.M., and then again at four. But at seven-thirty wake-up, it was sleeping almost as deeply as Jeremy.

Any other day, missing the bus and showing up late would have meant a simple chewing-out by the Principal, and maybe a detention or two. But today was the first day of Middle School, which meant picking classes for all of sixth grade. Jeremy was counting on getting into Music Appreciation, popularly known as "Snooze Patrol." It was a dream course — no homework, no tests — just show up in first period and listen to records. Best of all, Mr. DeRobis turned off the lights for better concentration on the music. So it was like getting an extra forty-five minutes of sleep every day. Besides, all of Jeremy's friends were going to be in that class.

But he was late, and Snooze Patrol was already full. He panicked, and his eyes flew to the list of classes that were still open.

"Pottery!" he croaked, signing up in a split-second decision. It was no Snooze Patrol, but how hard could it be to make ashtrays?

It was only when he showed up in Ms. Terranova's room that the truth hit. He had read the sheet wrong. This was not Pottery; it was Poetry. Furthermore, they didn't read it, they *wrote* it.

And no amount of begging and pleading to Ms. Terranova, the Principal, his parents, and God, could get him out of it.

As Ms. Terranova put it, "Anybody who could see *Poetry* and read *Pottery* needs all the English courses he can get."

The results amazed everyone, including Jeremy Bloom.

PART
I

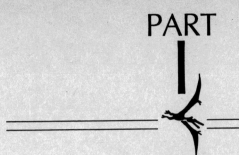

THE
PTERODACTYL
PERIOD

September 4 to October 30

THE
PTERODACTYL
PERIOD

If you call somebody Ms. Pterodactyl enough times in your mind, eventually it comes out your mouth.

That was how The Pterodactyl Period began exactly eight minutes into the first day of Ms. Terranova's Poetry class. Jeremy was trying to say, "Ms. Terranova, I don't belong in this class."

But it came out, "Ms. Pterodactyl — "

That was all it took. The other students howled with laughter. By the end of the day, the whole school knew about it, and Ms. Terranova couldn't take three steps without hearing someone from behind a door, yelling, *Heads up! It's a pterodactyl!*

It was written in Magic Marker on her classroom door. Someone slipped a small box of reptile food from the local pet shop into her mailbox in the office.

And at four o'clock, when she headed to the parking lot after a harrowing day, there it was, written in the dirt on the side of her car:

PTERODACTYL-MOBILE

It was amazing how many sixth graders knew how to spell *pterodactyl*.

Ms. Terranova never actually blamed Jeremy for starting the new nickname. So it's anybody's guess whether this had anything to do with her grading of his work. The poems of The Pterodactyl Period, the earliest of the five periods of Jeremy Bloom's poetic career, received a D minus. In fact, on the first monthly progress report, Ms. Terranova wrote:

The only thing that kept Jeremy from getting an F was the fact that he spelled his name right.

Was this the bitterness of a woman with giant dinosaur wings pinned to her coat? Or was Jeremy Bloom really a D-minus poet? The reader must decide.

I CAN'T CLEAN MY ROOM

I can't clean my room.

This may look completely chaotic to you,
Like a junk heap a hurricane just blasted through,
But it's neat in a way that is quite scientific,
It's orderly, sensible, truly terrific.
For instance, my homework goes under the hood
Of the race car I built that turned out not so good.
Clean socks are arranged in the box marked "keep out";
The dirty ones hang on the tip of the snout
Of my stuffed kangaroo, and its pouch is the place
For my glasses. (I'm growing some mold in the case.
It's a project for school, and I'm sure you'll agree
That we mustn't disturb it, or I'll get a D.)

I know that you're mad that I don't make my bed,
But it only gets mussed 'cause I work there instead
Of my desk, which I haven't seen since last November.
Oh, it's down there somewhere. I just don't remember
If it's under the town dump of shirts by the door,
Or the comic book library piled on the floor.
Do you need some more proof, or have you seen enough?
If I make one small change, then I won't find my stuff!

So I can't clean my room.

VITAL QUESTION

If a poem doesn't rhyme —
  How do you know
     It's a poem?

If it's about sunsets and flowers, well okay.

But some of them might be about termites, and rats,
Cockroaches, earwigs, bedbugs
  and silverfish,
Battalions of cooties,
  And are more like the exterminator's report
     Than a poem.

So how do you know it's a poem
  If it doesn't rhyme?

THE WORD

I'm packing my jeans
And my underwear, too
And I've found a ship bound for the sea.
For if Mom and Dad read
What I wrote on the wall,
It's going to be curtains for me.

It *is* just a Word,
It seemed harmless at first,
It has only four letters in all,
I did it in pencil,
It's not very dark,
And it's so nice and neat, and quite small.

But best to be safe,
So I'd better be off
To sail to those far distant lands.
For my one little Word
Is the kind of Word that
Will grow hair on the palms of your hands.

So it's me for the window,
And down to the yard,
Then away I go over the hill.
Of course, I could just
Turn my pencil around
And erase it — all right, then, I will!

WIDE AWAKE

The concert was awesome; it lasted so late! —

A great show like that leaves you totally wired!!!

I'm physically sharper than I ever was —

8

Big deal that school starts at a quarter to eight!

— My mother was worried that I would be tired

Too bad that my brain is converting to fuzz

9

z
z
z
z
z

APPEAL FOR A RAISE
IN ALLOWANCE

It seems clear to me that the normal progression
Of salary increases in my profession
Would indicate serious signs of recession
That lead to severe economic depression.

And so I request my parental relation
To give an immediate pay elevation
Which will give me cause for a wild celebration
To rattle the windows across this great nation

And stave off starvation.

Inflation.

NAME-CALLING

On Monday she was Christie, and
On Tuesday she was Krysti, and
On Wednesday she was Cristee, and
On Thursday she was Kristye, and
On Friday she was Chrystey.

On not one single weekday
Was the spelling quite the same.

But on weekends, she was Bertha,
Because that was her real name.

BILLY RAE THE DENTIST

This is the tale of Billy Rae,
A guy who really earns his pae,
I have to see him Saturdae;
I think I'd rather run awae.

I know just what he's going to sae:
"You brush and floss, or you will pae.
"Your teeth will all fall out one dae,
"You gums will be in disarrae,

"And when you smile, you will displae
"A mouth chock-ful of tooth decae
"That I must drill and scrape awae."
Oh, how I hate you, Billy Rae!

WHY I WAS LATE

I was late for school on Monday,
I rolled in at half past nine,
Miss Hackensack demanded
An excuse; I gave her mine.

The house across the street blew up.
The rubble on our lawn
Was twelve feet deep! I worked all night!
I shoveled until dawn!

The school bus made me later!
It was hijacked on the hill.
Dave Brooks was taken hostage,
And I'm sure he's out there still!

Well, then I saw the crater,
And I had to go around it.
I never thought I'd see the school!
I'm quite amazed I found it!

The news made all the papers —
It's not my fault she missed it.
To illustrate this point, I dropped
Down to the ground and kissed it.

My teacher made a face and kicked me out into the hall.
They don't trust a guy at all!

13

I was late for school on Tuesday,
Though I ran the last half mile.
I gave Miss H. the reasons
In inimitable style:

My family are Druids,
And today was Stonehenge Day,
When we stand in groups of seven,
Sacrifice a goat, and pray.

We can't start till the sunrise,
But today, you know, is cloudy,
And did the sun come up or not?
The argument got rowdy.

We went to get the Druid Book
To search for ancient tips.
There was nothing under "cloudy,"
So we had to check "eclipse."

Through much interpretation
Between Dad and Uncle Gus,
By the time the clouds had broken,
I'd already missed the bus.

Miss Hackensack just stared at me, then laughed right
in my face.
There is no faith in this place!

14

I was late for school on Wednesday,
There was this atomic bomb,
Otherwise I would have made it,
And I had a note from Mom

Which explained so very clearly
Why I would be late to show,
'Cause around nuclear weapons
You just have to take it slow.

You'd better walk on tiptoe
And don't slam the door too hard.
(Did I mention that this bomb lay
Unexploded in our yard?)

We don't know how it got there —
Was it plane or sub or rocket?
I pondered this and jammed my mother's
Note into my pocket.

But in my rush to get to school
I dropped it in the mud.
To top it off, the Army says
Our bomb was just a dud.

She screamed and yelled and carried on, and said I was
a flake.
They should give a guy a break!

15

I was late for school on Thursday,
Though I sprinted eighteen blocks,
I gasped and told Miss H. about
The problem with the clocks.

An asteroid passed by the earth,
Through our magnetic shield,
Enveloping our planet in
A time-distortion field.

This threw off my alarm clock
In a most peculiar way.
According to the VCR,
It's quarter past today!

The beeper on my dad's new watch
Went off three hours too late,
And going by our microwave,
It's 1948!

Folks are mixed up, the traffic's nuts,
The airport's going squirrely,
The only one on time is me —
The rest of you were early!

She marched me to the principal, and then I really got
it.
(At first I thought she'd bought it.)

I was late for school on Friday
'Cause my sister saw a mouse
And she really hit the ceiling —
There was murder at our house!

Then my father had a tantrum —
You have never seen the like —
When he backed out of our driveway
Squashing flat my ten-speed bike.

I hardly even noticed when
He came in with the news,
For I'd just found out the hard way
There was oatmeal in my shoes.

And right when I was off to catch
The last bus in this town,
Petunia climbed a tree, and someone
Had to get her down.

I missed the bus because
I had to rescue that dumb cat,
I couldn't ride my bike to school —
We've just established that.

She turned bright red and shrieked, "I will have no more
lies from you!
This time — honest — it was true!

17

PART
II

THE STINKO-
SMOKESCREEN-
WHIZBANGER
PERIOD

October 31 to December 21

THE STINKO-
SMOKESCREEN-
WHIZBANGER
PERIOD

The Pterodactyl Period ended on October 30, as students fluttered around the school in all sorts of costumes. Jeremy and his two best friends, Michael and Chad, felt they were far too cool for dressing up, and decided instead to celebrate Halloween the way they had the last three years in elementary school — with the ceremonial booby-trapping of the Girls' washroom.

This year's explosive was a combination stink-bomb, smoke-bomb, and cherry-bomb. The three all agreed the device was brilliant. The deafening firecracker would set off the smoke-bomb, and at the same time break the container that released the smelly gas.

With Jeremy and Michael stationed as lookouts,

Chad played the part of the mad bomber. He hid just inside the entrance to the Boys' washroom next door, waiting for this year's victim.

Since Michael and Chad were both in Snooze Patrol class, and not Poetry, only Jeremy recognized the small bustling figure in the witch costume. Ms. Terranova was short and slight, and could easily be mistaken for an eighth-grade girl. Michael gave Jeremy the thumbs-up sign.

Horrified, Jeremy cried, *"No!"*

But in his hiding place, Chad heard it as "Now!" He leapt out of the Boys' room, lit the fuse, and before Jeremy could stop him, tossed the Stinko-Smokescreen-Whizbanger into the Girls'.

There was an enormous BOOM, a cry of shock, and Michael and Chad beat a hasty retreat down the hallway.

Jeremy later admitted that it was stupid to run in and try to rescue Ms. Terranova. At the time, it seemed like a way to make points with the teacher who was already angry with him for saddling her with the nickname *Pterodactyl*.

The incident created a grudge that lasted until Christmas. As for the poems of The Stinko-Smokescreen-Whizbanger Period, the D minuses lasted until Christmas, too. Was it shell-shock or bad writing? The reader will be the judge.

HONESTY IS NOT ALWAYS THE BEST POLICY

Dear Aunt Matilda,

To thank you for this awesome shirt's the reason I am writing.
Translation: To wear it feels like forty thousand fire ants are
biting.

It's really a fantastic gift, a very stylish thing.
Translation: When it was last in fashion, good old George III
was king.

The fabric is amazing; I don't know how they make it.
Translation: I'm pretty sure that some poor horse is running
around naked.

The color's great. Just yesterday I showed it to the bunch.
Translation: The girls all laughed, and Andy Romanelli lost
his lunch.

And what a fit! I thought that it was custom-made for me!
Translation: And fifteen sumo wrestlers round a spreading
chestnut tree!

So thank you once again; this was exactly what I wanted.
Translation: I love humiliation! I get off on being taunted!

Yours very sincerely,
Translation: Next year send money,

Jeremy

PROFESSION

There's no sense planning to be
A dinosaur hunter.
They're extinct —
Which doesn't mean they smell bad.
It means they're dead.
(The dinosaurs, not the hunters.)
So they'd be wasting their time
(The hunters, not the dinosaurs.)
Better be an accountant.

NEGOTIATING BEDTIME

Mom came in at nine P.M.,
I figured I'd start high.
I gave her half-past midnight —
Hey, it was worth a try.

She jumped it to nine-thirty,
So I dropped to twelve-fifteen,
I had to give a little;
Look how sensible she's been!

She said, "Nine forty-five,"
I countered, "Twelve-o-seven-thirty,"
Negotiated settlements
Are always down and dirty.

I mentioned it's one-thirty
Before Alvin goes to bed.
(Of course he looks like someone
From *Night of the Living Dead*.)

Mom dug in. I begged and pleaded,
"Just one more half hour!"
It's hard to bulldoze someone
Who already holds full power.

She offered up eleven,
With the TV off by ten,
I accepted with conditions,
And we started off again.

Like, midnight on the weekends,
And I had a perfect reason
To ask the same for Monday nights
Throughout the football season.

She had no answer; this had put her
On the ropes for real.
I threw in garbage take-out;
And she folded. *"It's a deal!"*

TAKING A FALL

I'm taking a fall
'Cause I had the gall
To play ball
In the mall
With Paul.

One call
From the mom of the girl with the doll
That we hit with the ball.
That was all.

She was small —
Almost too young to crawl —
But could she ever bawl
Over one lousy doll!

Then Paul
Took off down the hall
To the can, where he hid in a stall,
Leaving me with my back to the wall.

I'm taking a fall.

ANSWERING MACHINE
MESSAGE

Hello, you've reached the Bloom house,
But we can't take your call,
We're either very busy,
Or we're not home at all.

We're probably out shopping,
Or maybe on a trip —
A flying visit to Peru;
Perhaps we've taken ship

To some exotic port of call,
Like Fiji, London, Rome,
Or Hackensack, New Jersey.
That's why there's no one home.

We could be in the south of France,
Relaxing in the sun,
Or climbing up Mount Everest —
I hear that's sort of fun.

Or maybe in Australia,
Helping shepherds tend their sheep.
But we'll be calling back,
So leave your number at the beep.

EQUIPMENT FAILURE

I don't think I am making an unreasonable request
To ask that my machinery be of the very best.
I should not have to waken in the morning just to find
Severe equipment failure of a truly nasty kind.
I ought to have an upgrade right from the very start,
Mechanical replacement — my bike just fell apart!

FOR YOUR OWN GOOD

"It's for your own good," means you'll hate it —
It sounds, tastes, and smells really bad —
It probably hurts — it's unpleasant —
It makes you unbearably sad —

It lies and it steals — it's a cheater —
It's everything awful in one.
It's boring — it's vile — it's a loser —
The worst thing you ever have done.

It brings on disease — it's obnoxious —
It causes your engine to stall —
It's sickening, evil, disgusting —
You aren't going to like it at all.

Oh, sure, you accept it. You have to
Knuckle under. You're not made of wood.
But nothing could be more depressing
Than hearing, "It's for your own good."

DEFINITION

A poem.

Rhyme salad,
Chopped by the word processor,
Garnished with pictures,
Sprinkled with adjectives,
Tossed by a poet-chef.
Lettuce, onions, tomatoes, images —

A poem.

THE OLYMPIAN

I'm going to practice every day,
I'm going to train like mad,
I'll be the best Olympian my country ever had.
I've got the guts, the will to win,
Tenacity, I think.
There's just one thing to hold me back —
At every sport I stink.

I'll start with gold in pole vault,
Run and plant the stick and fly —
(I'm asking the officials not to put the bar so high.)
And then I'll throw the discus,
I've got confidence galore.
Why, just last week when practicing
I shattered our glass door.

And for the pool I'm eating right,
And keeping fit and trim.
To get that breaststroke medal, I might even learn to
                                        swim.
Of course, I'll sweep the track events
Just like a shooting star,
I'll even win the marathon —
I hope it's not too far!

I'm trying out for basketball
'Cause it's my favorite sport.
I know that I can help the team — although I'm very
short.

In boxing I'll accept a bronze,
I don't expect the gold.
My sister knocked me out last week;
She's only three years old.

I'll win the weight-lifting events
Although I'm not too strong,
Those medals are so heavy, I'll be *huge* before too long.

And as for fencing, all opponents
Better be "en garde,"
I almost stabbed my dad last week
While training in the yard.

I'll shatter cycling records.
My opponents, to their sorrow,
Don't realize my training wheels are coming off
tomorrow.

And to this stack of medals
I'll just have to add one more:
Decathlon — I can't miss, since I've won
Every sport before.

I'll be a hit. There's just one snag
I have to work out first.
Of all the people trying out, I know I'll be the worst.
I almost hear the anthem,
Yes, my life's in perfect synch,
Except for that one tiny flaw —
At every sport I stink.

PART
III

THE WRONG
BOX PERIOD

January 2 to March 8

III

THE WRONG
BOX PERIOD

By this time, the D minuses had come to the attention of Jeremy's mother. Mrs. Bloom decided that before the holiday break, it would be a good idea for Jeremy to give Ms. Terranova a nice Christmas present as a peace offering. The money for the silk scarf came from Jeremy's allowance, which really cut into the joke presents he was able to buy for Michael and Chad.

On Christmas morning, Chad phoned to thank Jeremy for the whoopee cushion. The whole family had fallen for it, even the dog, and they were all suitably disgusted. The gift was a hit.

"Yeah, glad you liked it," said Jeremy. "I've got to get off the phone now. Michael's probably going to call soon. I got him something great, too — fake barf. Wait till you see it. It's totally real!"

But when Michael called, it was to ask, "What am I supposed to do with a lady's scarf?"

"Oh, that's just a mistake," laughed Jeremy. "The scarf was for Ms. Pterodactyl."

"So who got *my* present?"

The truth was bitter. If Michael had the scarf, that meant the plastic vomit had gone to Ms. Terranova. Come to think of it, he *did* remember a moment of confusion, since the flat square boxes had looked quite similar during the wrapping. But he had been so sure. . . .

Perhaps Michael summed up The Wrong Box Period best when he said: "I guess if you want to get on your teacher's good side, you should give her the scarf, not the barf."

Starting January 2, the parade of D minuses continued. Plastic vomit or literary merit? It is for the reader to discern.

THE BEAUTIFUL DAY

It's snowing, it's slushy, it's lousy, it's gray,
What joy to crawl back into bed for the day!
It's windy, it's slippery, it's misty, it's bad,
It's one of the worst days that we've ever had.
It's miserable, awful, disgusting out there,
The dampness and mist fuzzifies all my hair.
But to me it's like glorious sunshine in May,
A charming, delicious, delectable day,
Because Marcy, the beauty, the Queen of the Prom,
Has slipped on the ice and gone down like a bomb.

CERTAINLY I DID MY HOMEWORK

I.

Certainly I did my homework.
It's in plastic to protect
It from damage. I'll produce it
Soon for maximum effect.

Like when there's a lull at recess,
Or a ring around the moon,
I will step up with my homework —
You are going to see it *soon*.

And I think it's somewhat better
Than the others in the class,
I don't want to be a show-off — no,
I only want to pass.

II.

Why don't I just present it?
Well, this is how I feel:
I want the moment to be right.
I think the class should kneel.

The lights should probably be dimmed,
Tuxedos might be rented,
Conditions have to be ideal
When art forms are presented.

So when you see it — very soon! —
I'm sure you'll be impressed.
I like to think my work is just
A cut above the rest.

III.

For those of you who think perhaps
My homework isn't done
Because I stayed out late last night,
And traded work for fun,

Let me assure you, certainly,
That you are very wrong.
That masterpiece, my homework,
Will be shown before too long.

IV.

Well, no — I can't produce it
Just this second, as you'll hear.
It's not exactly with me,
But don't worry! It's quite near!

I wouldn't have to fret, or make
Excuses anymore
If I just had that table from
The hall by our front door,

It's got my father's car keys,
And my mother's Sunday bonnet.
Oh, how I need that table,
Because my homework's on it!

SEASONS

As everybody knows full well,
Because it is the rule,
Summer's for holidays, swimming, and fun,
And winter's for blizzards,
  freezing,
    heavy boots,
      fender benders,
       and school.

So it's one of life's misfortunes,
A terrible disaster,
That winter drags on day by day,
And summer goes faster,
  and faster,
    and faster,
      and faster,
       and faster.

NUTRITION REPORT

The minimum daily allowance
Of chocolate is now fourteen pounds,
Divided between Hershey Kisses,
Fudge, chocolate chip cookies, and Mounds.

Bazooka Joe gum is essential,
Tortilla chips make you much stronger,
Increase your intake of white sugar
So you can stay healthier longer.

For developing bones and good posture
It's obvious ice cream's the key,
Washed down with five gallons of cola,
Or 7-Up, not sugar-free.

Of course, you will need lots of fiber,
Like pretzels, and popcorn, and chips.
Make certain that nothing which grows in the ground
Is permitted to pass through your lips.

And this rule is terribly urgent:
We must be sure everyone eats a
Colossal amount of tomato, three-cheese,
Pepperoni and anchovy pizza.

SURGEON GENERAL'S NOTE:

It's probably a bad idea to do what this guy said.
It's excellent for gaining weight, and things like dropping dead.

44

CHORES

When you're tired from doing your schoolwork,
And there's something great on the TV,
They can't bear to see that you're idle,
They call out, "Please come and help me."
Then they give you a carrot, and tell you to grate it.
       I hate it!

You're about to go out to play baseball,
You're putting your cap on your head,
They pull you back in through the doorway,
And show you your nice unmade bed.
You'll soon be back in it, but they won't debate it.
       I hate it!

You're standing and drying the dishes,
You've swept the garage out today,
You figure you're well off the hook now,
They pat your sore back, and they say,
"We're moving the piano; please go in and crate it."
       I hate it!

GRIDIRON

My sister is annoying, she's an artist, not a sports fan,

So maybe that's a problem, but it's small if you

and she says our football jerseys have too much brown,

consider that it's Christmas, and we've yet to score a
touchdown!

REPORT CARD BLUES

My report card is a loathsome thing,
A triumph it is not,
It tells how I am flunking French,
My Math is not so hot.

I got a D in History,
I found the Grammar tough,
I bombed out bad at Reading,
And Geography was rough.

I have to show this to my folks
My future will be grim.
It's lucky I can point right to
A brilliant grade in Gym.

THE WHEELER-DEALER

Horsehead Nebula, Betelgeuse, Mars —
I can take you to the stars.

I've got a brand-new telescope,
It's from my Uncle Joe,
Though why he'd think I'd want the thing
I'm certain I don't know.

Well, Michael had those sneakers —
They're cool; they pump with air.
They cost about the same amount —
The trade was really fair.

But then I went to Howie's place.
The guy has his own phone!
It would be great to call up
All my friends while I'm alone.

See, Howie needed sneakers.
It was perfect — we swapped even,
And I was feeling mighty fine —
Till I ran into Steven.

You know those new Nintendo games —
You try to stay alive
While hanging from a burning bridge?
Well, Steven had all five.

I'd barely got the first of these
Into my VCR
When Simon broke the news
That he was selling his guitar.

I dealt for the guitar,
And he went off with his Nintendo.
I knew no notes, no chords, no keys,
And no diminuendo.

I panicked, made a stupid trade,
And that was how I got
This onyx Chinese checkers game
That Kevin's sister bought.

So I was really up the creek
Till I remembered Dan.
He's easily the world's most avid
Chinese checkers fan.

I called him, and it proved to me
That life is one big cycle.
He asked to trade a telescope
That he had swapped with Michael!

And so I hugged my telescope
That Uncle Joe had bought.
I wouldn't trade it for the world —
At least, probably not. . . .

Horsehead Nebula, Betelgeuse, Mars —
I can take you to the stars.

PART
IV

THE
FENDER-BENDER
PERIOD

March 11 to April 25

IV

THE
FENDER-BENDER
PERIOD

The fourth phase of Jeremy Bloom's body of work began on the day that Two-Lip McNasty, the Man-Eating Plant, defended his wrestling title against two sumo wrestlers and a guy with a hockey stick.

On that very day, Mr. Bloom decided that all his son needed was a better "work station." So when Jeremy should have been watching the big match, live from Papua, New Guinea, he was stuck in the furniture store, desk-shopping with his dad.

The desk was tied onto the roof of the car, and the chair sat wedged in the trunk, but the blotter and drawers had to be crammed into the backseat, blocking the rear view. So Jeremy acted as signal-man, since the car was parked in tight, and Mr. Bloom couldn't see anything coming from behind.

That's when Jeremy spotted it — the giant-screen TV in the window of the furniture store. The match was on, and there was Two-Lip McNasty, a sumo wrestler in each fist, bashing their heads together like two coconuts. Then he turned on the guy with the hockey stick.

"Yeah!" screamed Jeremy, punching both arms triumphantly into the air. But all Mr. Bloom saw was his signalman confidently waving him out into traffic. He put the car in gear and pulled out, just as a shiny new sports coupe was passing by in the curb lane.

CRUNCH!

Mr. Bloom's Buick plowed into the side of the sports car, crumpling the passenger door and spinning the vehicle around.

The driver jumped out, screaming. It was Ms. Terranova.

It probably didn't help matters any when Jeremy blurted, "Dad! You belted Ms. Pterodactyl!"

He looked into her car. The mileage counter on the dash read: 00000.7 — not even a mile. She was three blocks from the dealership in her brand-new car.

Two-Lip McNasty won his bout, the guy with the hockey stick ate it, and Jeremy got a D minus on every single poem during The Fender-Bender Period. It might have been the body of work — or maybe just the body work. It's up to the reader.

I'M FEELING VERY ILL TODAY

I'm feeling very ill today,
　　as anyone can see,
I'm suffering from heartburn,
　　and water on the knee,
A terrible congestion,
　　a chronic overbite,
It's totally a miracle
　　I made it through the night!

I'm sure I did some damage
　　the time I scraped my knee,
That thumb-sprain from Nintendo
　　is painful as can be.
I'm in the final stages
　　of sour-pickle breath.
It's obvious to anyone
　　I'm on the brink of death!

Too bad there's no new medicine,
　　no special magic pill
To cure this awful weakness.
　　I'm writing out my will,
And leaving all my stuff to
　　those who recognize my plight,
And think how sad a state I'm in —
　　a truly piteous sight!

I cannot walk across the room
      without a dizzy head.
I greatly fear the consequences
      should I leave my bed!
My fever rises higher
      as I lie here and I shiver,
I'm sure I have the mumps,
      and palpitations of the liver.

And measles, chicken pox, and flu
      all rolled up into one,
So you can bet this being sick
      is not a bit of fun!
And anyone who cares at all
      would look at me and say,
"Forget your big exam, poor dear!
      You're staying home today!"

POETRY IS IMAGES

Poetry is images,
It doesn't have to rhyme.
We think in full-blown metaphor,
We do it all the time.

The pattern made by sewage
  On the mighty Hudson River
    As seen by limpid moonlight
      From the George Washington bridge.

The grace of that big fullback
  As he thunders down the gridiron
    Till the defense finally traps him,
      And they squash him like a bug.

The neat concentric circles
  Drawn by the tail of Fido
    As you fill his bowl with scraps of stuff
      You wouldn't feed a dog!

That field of purple hyacinths,
  True harbingers of Springtime,
    With rich exotic perfume —
      How sweet to sneeze in mauve.

The polka dots of litter
　　Across the verdant landscape;
　　　A mighty nation's nourishment
　　　Is chocolate bars and chips.

　　We think in tidy simile,
　　We do it all the time,
　　Poetry is images —
　　It doesn't have to rhyme.

VOCABULARY

I think that today I'll invent a new word.
An adjective. See how you like it. It's *glurd*.

When something is *glurd*, it's especially nice,
Like chocolate, and hockey, Nintendo, and *flice*.

Of course I mean red *flice*, 'cause *flice* that are green
Are not *glurd* at all; they're depressingly *sveen*.

With *glurd flice*, not *sveen flice*, a guy's in great shape.
He can *wazzle*, *perfuffle*, *kazyme*, and *terflape*.

You wonder why I use new words like *kazyme*?
It's so I can get these dumb poems to rhyme.

THE GUEST LIST

It wouldn't be a party without McKenzie Schwartz,
And Oddball and his brother have recovered from their
warts.

Nasty
Reggie
Ivan the Veggie

Foghead
Steve
The guy who won't leave

Jerome, and Michael Stitsky, and his friend with the red
hair,
Have phoned to say they're bringing Mike's exploding
underwear.

Stan the Man
Dan McCann

Rhubarb
Jerry
Dingleberry

Garlic-breath Bavinsky has a cousin in from Boise.
We've warned our nearest neighbors that the party
might get noisy.

Electric Joe
Toothless Moe

Antenna-face Rice
Doctor Ice

Banana Crusher's coming, and the guy with see-through
sneakers,
Plus MoJo; he's the hippy with the floor-to-ceiling
speakers.

Balloon Man
Killer Van

Igor
Ugly
Wimpy McSnuggly

We've reinforced the basement so the concrete floor
won't crack,
When two-ton Harry does his dance and lands flat on his
back.

Vinnie the Zit
Mike Messerschmidt

Four-eyed Rick
Six-eyed Nick

For crowd control we're bringing in a dozen private eyes,
The hospital's on red alert in case somebody dies.

Bubba the Horse
Fred, of course

Les
Wes
Pizza Express

We're making party history, with nothing left to chance;
The White House sent the Presidential Pardon in
advance.

Mayday Ira Wuthers
Chico and his brothers

Myron Slate
Hey, wait!!!

Man, we forgot to ask the girls! There's not a single one!
I'm staying home. This boring party won't be any fun.

ANDREW AND ANDY

Andrew is an angel,
And Andy is a devil.
Andy never tells the truth,
But Andrew's on the level.

Andrew is a gentleman.
So very well-behaved.
Andy's who you look for
When you find the cat's been shaved.

Andrew's kind and neat,
And always gets a summer job.
Andy's mean and lazy,
And a veritable slob.

I know them inside out, I do,
They're very clear to see.
Andrew's good, and Andy's not —
And both of them are ME.

MEAN CUISINE

The worst thing in all of creation,
I'm telling you right off the bat,
Is dining at my Auntie Annie's,
It would make you spit up in your hat.
There's nothing more awful than that.

    Fleas' knees,
      yak cheese,
        canary beaks lightly stewed —

    What ever happened to good old food?

You sit at the table in horror,
And slip your fork down to the cat.
But what can you do with the stuff when
The animal turns you down flat?
There's nothing more awful than that.

    Flies' eyes,
      fish thighs,
        Cajun-style nostril of cow —

    What ever happened to decent chow?

If you manage to hide some beneath you,
It leaves a green stain on the mat.
Aunt Annie sees room on your plate then,
And says, "Have more filet of bat."
There's nothing more awful than that.

    Does' toes,
      eel's nose,
        chili con wolverine —

    What ever happened to fine cuisine?
    My Auntie Annie cooks *mean*.

A PERFECT AFTERNOON

It's a perfect afternoon
  For a creative guy like me.
I could hollow out a kayak
  From the Schnitzenbergers' tree.
I could carve a famous statue
  From the rock behind our house.
I was thinking of the Pietà,
  Or an eight-foot Mickey Mouse.
I could write an opera, operetta,
  Big best-seller, too.
There is no limit to the things
  That I could surely do.
I could cure the common cold,
  And blow a masterpiece in glass.
But I can't, because my father says
  I have to cut the grass.

BE PREPARED

This is Poetry class,
And I am supposed to be writing a poem.
I chew on my pencil;
I stare upward, seeking inspiration —
And count the holes in the ceiling.

Twelve holes by twelve holes in each white tile
(one-forty-four)
The room is twenty-two tiles by twenty-nine—
Six hundred and thirty-eight tiles!
Ninety-one thousand eight hundred
    and seventy-two holes!

But this is only one of thirty-eight classrooms!
Boasting three million four hundred and ninety-one
    thousand, one hundred and thirty-six Grade A
        government-inspected ceiling holes!

Divided by six hundred and twelve students,
Comes to five thousand seven hundred and four
    and a half each.

I won't have a poem when the bell rings,
But should the teacher want some dazzling stats—
I'll be ready.

IT'S ONLY A TREE

It's only a tree, and an ugly one, too,
And the fact is, it has to come down.
It blocks out the sun for each house on the street.
There's been a complaint from the town.

When Mom put up the tire swing
She checked the branch like anything,
Made sure our feet could reach the slope,
And then forgot to test the rope.
So when it broke, poor Mallory
Rolled right clear down to Highway 3.
The bus she almost hit head-on
Swerved right and jumped up on our lawn.
It sheared the hydrant off its post —
I think that's when I laughed the most —
The water shot up thirty feet
And hit the wires. It was neat.
Knocked out the electricity.
It was a special day for me.

I've got to save that tree!

It's only a tree, and its roots have gone wild;
They're into the Smiths' septic tank,
Their lawyer just called, said the smell is intense,
And the doghouse above it just sank.

When Rick Levine, the town's big pest,
Knocked down that giant hornet's nest,
We scattered fast, we took off quick,
And all the hornets followed Rick
Right through the Abernathys' yard.
(By now he's running pretty hard.)
He hit the line of drying clothes,
Picked up four pairs of panty hose,
But didn't falter in the race
With underwear wrapped round his face.
He kept on going past the school,
Dove right into the Wilsons' pool,
Which busted up their Sunday tea.
He treaded water, hornet-free.

How can we lose that tree?

It's only a tree, and it's lived long enough;
Dead branches are snarled in the eaves,
Just think of the bugs we won't have to fight off,
And next Fall we won't rake tons of leaves.

We knew our tree house was the best,
But Dad still put it to the test.
He had to check it out, he said,
If it caved in, we'd end up dead.
And he was right; I give him credit.
It happened just the way he said it.
He climbed right up and jumped about,
The floor gave way, and he fell out,
A low branch snagged him by the seat;
He hung there like a slab of meat.
It was the biggest news in town,
It took the cops to get him down.
It's just like yesterday to me,
Imprinted on my memory.

I'm going to miss that tree!

PART
V

THE
TARZAN
PERIOD

April 26 to June 14

V

THE
TARZAN
PERIOD

Jeremy signed up for the Spring play in a last-ditch effort to pull up his Poetry grade. The Fender-Bender Period had pretty much ruled out the A's and B's, but a low C was not out of reach if he could really impress Ms. Terranova, who was the play's director and a real drama fan.

The play was *Tarzan*, and Jeremy's part was small but vital. One of the gym's climbing ropes had been painted green to be the ape man's swinging vine. Jeremy's job was to stand on a raised platform in the wings and hold the rope until it was time for Tarzan to make his big entrance. It was a stupid part, but the best he could hope for since Ms. Terranova was in charge of casting. He was lucky he wasn't the peel off the apes' bananas.

Ms. Terranova directed from a clump of cardboard reeds dead center on the stage. That way she could see all the actors, but be invisible to the audience behind the painted scenery.

On opening night, with the gym packed with parents, teachers, and the entire school board, Jeremy's boredom reached its zenith. He had been up late, filling his pockets with itching powder to sprinkle on Tarzan just before he swung out into the spotlight. It was a cruel joke, but Tarzan was Michael, and he and Michael always forgave each other.

Jeremy was never sure exactly how it happened, but he fell asleep at the rope. And when he awakened, he was airborne. Clawing frantically at the "vine," he swung out over the stage, screaming, *"He-e-e-e-lp!"* at the astonished crowd. A desperate grab with his windmilling legs caught the reeds at center stage. Instead of stopping him, the scenery lifted off and went with him, leaving a crouching Ms. Terranova, her hind end raised and pointed at the audience, in full view.

Ms. Terranova made a grab at Jeremy, but succeeded only in upsetting his balance on the rope. He swung upside down, itching powder sprinkling from his pockets, blanketing the stage and half the audience.

Jeremy later pointed out that it was Ms. Terranova's fault, and not his, that the school had to pay for the dry-cleaning and de-itching of a hundred and forty-seven suits and dresses. Still, he was relieved to get D minuses throughout The Tarzan Period. Which may or may not have had something to do with Ms. Terranova's sudden allergy to itching powder. As always, the decision is in the hands of the reader.

THE NEUTRON PANTS RAP

(for experienced rappers only)

Yo, Mom, you know what everybody thinks?
My whole Fall wardrobe really stinks.
I thought last night while chillin' out at Fred's,
Hey, if you want to be hype, you've got to have the
threads.

Now, Fred's Mom's really on the ball,
So yesterday she took him over to the mall,
And got his Christmas present in advance,
A pair of baggy, heavy-duty, funky neutron pants.

Those neutron pants, they're fly, they're cool, they're
fine,
A steal at only eighty-seven ninety-nine.
While I'm on my butt like a total sap,
Home's fronting in his neutrons, working on his rap.
So Mom, it's no snowjob, here's the scoop:
I've got to be accepted by my own peer group.
You've got to lend me the juice, you've got to give me
the chance
To get some baggy, heavy-duty, funky neutron pants.

(Thanks, Mom, you're the best,
They're looking nasty under my atomic vest.)

I was walking through the school, dazzling all the chicks,
Acting fresh en route to auto shop in period six,
When I saw that girl Loretta, she was looking at me,
I knew she was impressed by my haberdashery.
And when we got to class, I knew it was my day;
We got to work together on the Chevrolet.
I worked up my nerve and asked her to the dance,
And she dumped a can of grease all down my neutron
pants.

The guy at the laundromat said, "No way.
That stain is going to be there until doomsday."
I can't believe Loretta — even if she'd missed me!
I tell you, Slick, it's cold the way the lady dissed me!
I tried to spread the word that the stain was cool,
But Loretta blabbed the story all over school.
I think I'm going to have to relocate to France
In my baggy, heavy-duty, funky, greasy neutron pants.

(*A vendre: les pantalons neutron d'Amerique —
Très chic.*)

THE BALLAD OF ARABELLA HOPP

The prettiest girl in our whole school
Is Arabella Hopp,
And every time she smiles at me,
I think my heart will stop.

The guys all flock to be with her
Like bees around the honey.
Big Larry's on the football team,
And Joe's got piles of money,

And Tom is great at hockey,
He's the hero of the rink,
Bill Ferguson is handsome —
Or that's what people think,

Jeff Williams is a ladies' man,
As anyone can see,
But out of all these winners,
Arabella Hopp chose me.

HOW TO WAKE A GUY
FOR SCHOOL

When morning is upon the world
At seven on the clock,
A person must be wakened
So as not to suffer shock.

You never pound upon the door
And yell, "It's time to rise!"
Oh, be humane, have mercy.
Get the sleep out of his eyes

By playing soothing music,
And avoiding any mental
Exertion that might cause a strain.
You must be kind and gentle.

You never holler "Up and out,
And stand upon your feet!"
The treatment should be tentative,
And delicate, and sweet.

He's in a fragile state, you know,
From going late to bed.
So don't be bright and cheery —
It might detonate his head.

He knows he must get up for school;
It's been that way for years.
But, oh, how mean to let your calls
Assault his weary ears!

And don't be cruel enough to let
That loud alarm clock bleep.
(If you had any pity,
You would let the poor soul sleep.)

ON THE BRINK

I'm on the brink.

I can't get a drink.
I think
I got zinc
In the sink.

(It's pink.
Does it ever stink!)

There's a kink —
You might say a link.
Yesterday I got ink
On Mom's mink;
Today I got zinc
In her sink.
In a wink.
I'm a fink
Who should slink
To the clink.

I'm on the brink.

MY CHAUFFEUR

My sister got her license,
And the future's looking sour.
She backs out of our driveway
At a hundred miles an hour!

She gives me lifts; I swear
My stomach's never been so tight.
We screech around the neighborhood
Well past the speed of light!

She's on and off the sidewalk,
Windows open, tape deck pounding,
As people run for cover,
Her obnoxious horn is sounding.

The whiplash doesn't bother me —
Nor even fear of death.
But on the way to school today
She sideswiped my friend Seth.

His bike's okay, but man oh man,
The guy is still in shock!
I should refuse to ride with her,
But then I'd have to *walk*!

AMBITION

Just because other explorers have already discovered
The good places,
And the only spots left are cold,
Or hot,
Or dull,
Or have isthmuses
(Whatever they are),
Doesn't mean you can't make
A very nice, modest discovery
At, say, the South Pole,
And they can name it after you:
Jeremy's Land.
Jeremyville.
New Jeremy.
South Jeramerica.
It has a nice ring to it.

I DIDN'T

I *didn't* mess the kitchen up,
I *didn't* lose my gloves,
I *didn't* smash the china horse —
The one my mother loves.

I *didn't* smear black fingerprints
On pristine, off-white walls,
I *didn't* turn the bathtub
Into Niagara Falls.

I *didn't* hide my vegetables
Under the kitchen mat.
I *didn't* break a window.
I *didn't* bean the cat.

There is an endless list of evil
Things I *didn't* do,
Like not making crank phone calls,
Or cooking sister stew,

Or causing giant tidal waves
To crash upon the shore.
I *didn't* drop an atom bomb
And start a major war.

I'm on my best behavior —
Pure and innocent at heart,
But I *didn't* do my homework,
So I'm doomed right from the start.

SCIENCE

In science there's this subatomic particle—
the lepton.

It doesn't seem important since my poor pet ant
got stepped on.

I PULLED AN "A"

I pulled an "A" in math today
It took a bit of work,
I highly recommend it, though —
Your parents go berserk.

It's not enough to buy you stuff
To celebrate your grade,
They also grant you privileges
For this great mark you've made.

Your mom cooks all your favorite foods,
Your dad makes "genius" jokes,
An "A" in math sure makes it tough
To recognize your folks.

Your sister does the dishes, and
Your brother rakes the yard,
I'll get an "A" again one day —
That's if it's not too hard.

NO BORING PARTS ALLOWED

I.

The movie was a thriller;
   I was frozen in my chair;
The city was in ruins —
   there was gunfire everywhere;
The rain came down for six straight weeks;
   the tanks were mired in mud;
A maniac was loose in town;
   the gutters ran with blood.
The hero was in trouble;
   he was hanging by a thread.
There were thirty thousand cannons
   aimed directly at his head.
Below him was the heroine,
   with nitro at her throat.
Their chances of survival
   seemed decidedly remote.
He jumped a measly sixty feet —
   somehow the cannons missed him.
He freed the leading lady,
   they went off and then she — *kissed him?*

Time out — hang on — hold up!
By some incredible mischance
This real artistic action flick
Turned into a romance!
It killed the classy things with which
This movie was endowed,
And broke my Number One strict rule:
No boring parts allowed.

II.

The book was fascinating;
　I just couldn't put it down.
A nasty gang of spies was centered
　in this little town.
The author was a genius
　with the deepest bag of tricks.
There had been a hundred murders!
　I was only on page six!
I think it was the car chase
　with the good guys and the crooks
That made me phone to order
　all the author's other books.
A writer of this stature,
　I am quick to emphasize,
Should dry-clean his tuxedo
　to accept the Nobel Prize.

The hero lay in hiding,
   one last bullet in his gun.
There followed a description
   of — the *setting of the sun?*
         I skipped ahead — it was still setting
         After fourteen pages.
         To get through this dumb sunset
         I would have to read for ages!
         The book went for recycling,
         'Cause I have always vowed
         That I would never compromise:
         No boring parts allowed.

III.

I sat awake at two A.M.,
   glued solid to the screen;
It was the greatest TV show
   that I had ever seen.
The Comet-Master, Vorgon,
   went careening past the stars,
Pursued by blaster-demons
   from the government of Mars.
The earth had disappeared,
   and with it, all the human race,
And Vorgon had to find it
   somewhere lost in hyperspace.

91

At station break I phoned
   to thank the guys at Channel 3.
When I got back, the Martians
   set their guns on "fricassee."
The ship was hit! The hull caved in!
   And things were getting gory,
When Master Vorgon lectured on —
   the moral of the story?
            You interrupt the fighting and
            The killing and the strife
            To have some actor talk about
            The meaning of all life?
            I phoned them back and told them off.
            I'm not ashamed; I'm proud.
            When will these people ever learn?
            No boring parts allowed.

EPILOGUE

Forty-four D minuses average out to a final grade of D minus. No bell curve. It is impossible to say just how much Jeremy learned in his year with Ms. Terranova, since his first and last efforts, and all those in between, received exactly the same grade.

It is interesting, though, that Jeremy commented at the end that Poetry class was "not as boring as I thought." In fact, he found the writing part "kind of fun," and intended to continue. Next year, Ms. Terranova was offering a seventh-grade course in novel writing. If a few poems could do all this to the infamous Ms. Pterodactyl, Jeremy was sure he could come up with a D-minus novel that would totally blow her away.

Only, she wouldn't be Ms. Terranova anymore. On the last day of class, she told her students that she was going to be married that summer, and was planning to use her new husband's name. When she returned in September, she would be Mrs. Stegowitz.

As Jeremy left Poetry class for the very last time, he gave her his most sincere good wishes: "Have a nice summer, Mrs. Stegosaurus." By Labor Day, the whole school knew.

GRADING SCALE

A+	Excellent
A	Very Good
B	Good
C	Satisfactory
D	Poor
D–	Jeremy Bloom

About the Authors

Bernice Korman and Gordon Korman make up one of the only mother-and-son poetry-writing teams in the world today. Gordon's first book, *This Can't Be Happening at Macdonald Hall!*, was written for a seventh-grade English project. Bernice entered the business when Gordon conned her into typing it for him. Bernice lives in Thornhill, Ontario, with her husband, and sometimes with Gordon, when he's not at his New York apartment.

Gordon has written seventeen other books for Scholastic, the latest of which is *The Twinkie Squad*.